THE
SAC AND FOX
INDIANS

THE JUNIOR LIBRARY OF
AMERICAN INDIANS

THE
SAC AND FOX
INDIANS

Melissa McDaniel

CHELSEA JUNIORS
a division of CHELSEA HOUSE PUBLISHERS

ON THE COVER: Detail from a painting by George Catlin showing the Sac and Fox warring with the Teton Sioux.

FRONTISPIECE: A painting by George Catlin of Whirling Thunder, the oldest son of Black Hawk.

CHAPTER TITLE ORNAMENT: An animal design from a woven bag made by the Sac and Fox.

English-language words that are italicized in the text can be found in the glossary at the back of the book.

Chelsea House Publishers
EDITORIAL DIRECTOR Richard Rennert
EXECUTIVE MANAGING EDITOR Karyn Gullen Browne
COPY CHIEF Robin James
PICTURE EDITOR Adrian G. Allen
CREATIVE DIRECTOR Robert Mitchell
ART DIRECTOR Joan Ferrigno
PRODUCTION MANAGER Sallye Scott

The Junior Library of American Indians
SENIOR EDITOR Martin Schwabacher

Staff for THE SAC AND FOX INDIANS
ASSISTANT EDITOR Catherine Iannone
EDITORIAL ASSISTANTS Sydra Mallery, Erin McKenna
ASSISTANT DESIGNER Lydia Rivera

3 5 7 9 8 6 4

Library of Congress Cataloging-in-Publication Data

McDaniel, Melissa.
The Sac and Fox Indians / Melissa McDaniel.
   p. cm. — (The Junior library of American Indians)
Includes index.
        0-7910-1670-6
        0-7910-2034-7 (pbk.)
1. Sauk Indians—History—Juvenile literature. 2. Sauk Indians—Social life and customs—Juvenile literature. 3. Fox Indians—History—Juvenile literature. 4. Fox Indians—Social life and customs—Juvenile literature. [1. Sauk Indians. 2. Fox Indians. 3.Indians of North America.] I. Title. II. Series.   94-44785
E99.S23M34 1995   CIP
977'.00497'3—dc20   AC

CONTENTS

Sac and Fox warriors
painted their faces as a
sign of bravery and skill
in hunting and warfare.

Chapter 1

Brothers of the Mississippi Valley

Long ago, the Great Spirit informed the Sac people and the Fox people that they should think of each other as brothers and sisters. They were told to watch over each other and live near one another in harmony. The Great Spirit had chosen a special place for the Sac and Fox to live, where their friendship could thrive. The two tribes wandered for many years, looking for that special place, but wherever they settled, other Native American tribes or European settlers forced them out. Finally, they arrived in the fertile valley that the Great Spirit had selected for them. Here, as friends, they could live and *prosper.*

This is how the Sac and Fox explain how they came to settle along the Mississippi and Rock rivers in what is now northern Illinois and southern Wisconsin. The Sac and Fox, although often considered one group, are actually two distinct tribes. In their original homeland in eastern Michigan, the Sac and Fox had been friendly neighbors and trading partners. They shared many traditions and beliefs and had similar languages. Their alliance grew stronger as they became threatened by other groups moving into their region.

In the 17th century, Europeans began building settlements along the East Coast. The Sac and Fox were affected by the European invasion of the Americas long before they actually had contact with settlers. As the newcomers built their homes and towns and cleared land for farming, they forced Native Americans to move west. But wherever the displaced tribe settled, there was another tribe already residing on that land. Warfare and *skirmishes* commonly resulted.

In the middle of the 17th century, the Sac and Fox encountered members of the Iroquois tribes that lived in present-day New York State. The Iroquois had been trading beaver furs to European merchants since the

Sac and Fox warriors battle members of the Ojibwa tribe in Lake Superior. When the Native Americans were pushed west by the expansion of the United States, fighting often ensued as tribes were forced to compete for land.

beginning of the century. After decades of active hunting, few beavers remained in Iroquois territory. The Iroquois had to look for hunting grounds farther west, fighting other tribes to gain access to their territory. When the Iroquois, who were fierce warriors, began moving into eastern Michigan, the Sac and Fox decided to avoid fighting and leave their homeland. They headed west and settled in present-day Wisconsin.

In their new location, the Sac and Fox established friendly relations with some local tribes, and they began trading with French merchants. Before long, however, the Fox became angry with the French for trading

After leaving their homeland in eastern Michigan, the Sac and Fox settled along the Mississippi and Rock rivers. Their largest village was Saukenuk.

with the Teton Sioux Indians, who were enemies of the Fox. The Teton Sioux had to pass through Fox territory in order to reach French trading posts, and fighting often erupted between the two tribes.

The French did not want the Fox interfering with their trade with other tribes, so they began attacking the Fox. Although the Sac wanted to maintain friendly relations with the French, they felt compelled to aid their Fox allies. In 1733, the French attempted to destroy the Fox villages and drive the tribe from the region. The Fox sought protection in the Sac villages, and the French attacked both tribes. Together, the Sac and the Fox defeated the French, but they decided to move once again to avoid further skirmishes. They traveled south and settled along the Mississippi and Rock rivers, the place they believed they were destined to dwell.

The Mississippi Valley was rich and bountiful and provided the Sac and Fox with everything they needed. Along the river lay a fertile prairie that made excellent farmland. The Sac and Fox plowed this land and planted hundreds of acres of corn. Harvests were usually so plentiful that the Indians had extra corn to sell to traders. Nearby, there were fields of blue grass where the Indians' horses could graze. The Sac and Fox lived along a section of rapids in the Mississippi that teemed with fish. Near the river, many springs gushed clear, refreshing water. The forests were abundant with berries, fruits, and nuts.

The many animals that lived in this lush countryside supplied the Sac and Fox with food and skins for their clothing. Beavers, otters, and muskrats frolicked in the streams. Deer skittered through the woods, which

In this 19th-century engraving, Indians canoe near Fort Howard in Green Bay, Wisconsin. During the 17th and 18th centuries, the Sac and Fox made their homes along the shores of the Green Bay.

were also home to bears and raccoons. Farther west, on the prairie, herds of elk and buffalo grazed.

The Sac and Fox were reputed to be the best hunters in the Mississippi and Missouri river valleys. Each year they traded thousands of dollars worth of pelts to the French, Spanish, and British in exchange for horses, guns, animal traps, cooking utensils, blankets, and other goods.

The Sac and Fox lived contentedly in the valley where the Great Spirit had led them. But they would not live there for long before their security would again be threatened—this time by the newly formed United States of America. ▲

The Bad Axe River
flows through the
fertile territory that
was once home to
the Sac and Fox.

Chapter 2

The Rhythm of the Seasons

During their many happy years spent living along the Mississippi, the Sac and Fox followed a yearly cycle of hunting, farming, feasting, and trading. Coordinating their lives with the rhythm of the seasons, they were able to provide for all their needs.

The Sac and Fox lived in villages scattered along the rivers and streams that flowed into the Mississippi. These towns consisted of lodges—large buildings that each housed a few families—arranged in rows along wide streets. The Sac's main village, Saukenuk, impressed nearly everyone who visited with its size and orderliness. It contained more than 100 lodges housing as many as 3,000 people, more than half of the total Sac population at the time.

The lodges built by the Sac and Fox were often 40 to 60 feet long and 20 feet wide. Wooden poles were used to make a sturdy frame that was covered with large pieces of elm bark to keep the rain out.

This centuries-old drawing of an Indian village shows a neatly laid out town similar to those of the Sac and Fox.

Inside, skins and blankets were spread over sleeping benches that ran along the walls. Underneath the benches, people stored their possessions. A row of cooking fires—one for each family—stretched down the center of the lodge.

Sac and Fox women tended the hundreds of acres of crops that surrounded the villages. In May and June, the women planted beans, squash, melons, and pumpkins, as well as their most important crop—corn. Corn could be eaten straight off the cob or used to make soup. It could also be dried and pounded into meal to use when there were no fresh vegetables. The Sac and Fox also liked to put kernels of corn on hot rocks to make popcorn for the children. Besides farming, women gathered the nuts, fruits, berries, and honey that could be found in abundance near their homes and collected bark to make the lodges.

Most of the men spent the summer hunting and fishing. In the nearby forests, hunters would catch muskrat, raccoon, beaver, and rabbit. In the vast prairies across the Mississippi, they hunted buffalo and elk. These animals were particularly important to the Sac and Fox because they provided much more than food. The animal skins were used to make clothing and storage containers. The bones were used to make tools.

Some men traveled north to an area where lead, an important mineral, could be found. The metal lay near the surface of the ground, so the Sac and Fox could dig it out easily. Sometimes the Indians made decorations from the lead, but more often they exchanged it for the *manufactured* goods brought by the white traders.

By August, the crops were ripe and the vines were bursting with luscious fruits and vegetables, and the hunters, miners, and fishermen returned to their villages for the harvest. This was a joyous time as everyone came together to share what they had caught or grown. They would *indulge* in feasts day after day, enjoying their good fortune in living in such a bountiful area.

The Sac and Fox celebrated the harvest with great festivals, during which people competed in horse races and other games. In one of these games, the *forerunner* of lacrosse, the participants used a stick with a pouch on the end to carry and throw a ball, trying to get it downfield and into the opponents' goal. Hundreds of young men would play this game at one time on a vast stretch of prairie as long as 300 yards. Many of the spectators would wager on the outcome of the games and races, contributing to the excitement of the celebrations.

The Sac and Fox played an early version of the game now called lacrosse in which hundreds of players competed at once.

By early September, the last of the crops were harvested and a tribal council was held. The council assigned winter hunting grounds to different groups and decided on the date that everyone would leave the village. As that day grew near, canoes were packed with the weapons and traps needed to hunt. Before the Sac and Fox left their villages, they stored a *cache* of dried fruit, squash, and corn in the ground. Those too old to travel stayed behind with a few young men to look after them. Everyone else dispersed in small groups to the different hunting sites, where they would live in temporary camps. As the frigid winter months ensued, there was less game to catch, and the Indians spent the worst of the winter tucked away in their huts, protected from the cold and snow outside.

The Sac and Fox returned to their permanent villages with the first signs of spring, usually in April. There they uncovered the food supply they had carefully stored, enjoying the dried fruits and vegetables that had been so rare during the harsh winter. Men repaired any damage done to the lodges during the winter, and women prepared to plant the year's crops.

Every spring, women tilled the fields using shoulder bones of buffalo or deer. Over time, the soil had become soft and easy to work and the harvests were usually plentiful, producing more than enough to feed all the people. They traded the surplus to neighboring whites.

The harvests were shared among everyone in the village, and no one was ever allowed to go hungry if someone else had food. Black Hawk, a great 19th-century Sac leader, explained, "If we have corn and meat, and know of a family that have none, we divide with them. If we have more blankets than sufficient, and others have not enough, we must give to them that want."

Along with the rhythm of the passing years, this feeling of responsibility toward one another provided the Sac and Fox with a sense of security and permanence. ▲

Chapter 3

The Cycle of Life

T he Sac and Fox based their society upon respect for each other and for the world around them. They commemorated each stage of a person's life, giving every individual a strong sense of connection with the past and the future.

Every Sac and Fox belonged to a large family group called a clan. The Sac had 12 clans, including Bear, Bald Eagle, Thunder, Sturgeon, and Swan. The Fox had at least eight clans, including Wolf, Bear, Elk, and Black Bass. According to the Sac and Fox, each clan was descended from a single person who had sought a vision and was visited by a manitou, or a spirit, in the form of the

Sac and Fox babies were carried in cradleboards, which could be strapped to their mother's back or set down beside her while she worked.

23

thing the clan was named after. In this vision, the ancestor learned what objects to put in a sacred pack that would have special healing powers for the members of that clan. The pack consisted of such items as animal teeth, claws, and eagle feathers.

Twice a year, the clan members held a special ceremony honoring the powers of the pack. The more elaborate of these took place in the summer and involved feasting and dancing. The Indians would sing, pray, and retell the story of the original vision and the sacred pack. This ceremony reminded the manitou of what it had promised the clan's ancestor and what powers it had granted in the vision. It also reminded the clan members of their obligation to the manitou and their responsibilities to each other.

The Sac and Fox had another form of social organization besides the clans. When a baby was born, he or she was assigned to one of two groups, either black or white. A family's firstborn child was assigned to one group and the second child to the other group and so on, alternating through the siblings.

The clans and the black and white groups helped everyone in the tribe feel connected to everyone else. Because no person could marry someone from their own clan, every family had connections to other clans. In addition, many games and ceremonies were organized according to the black and white groups so that hostilities would not arise along clan lines.

Religion was a vital part of daily life for the Sac and Fox. They believed that each person, animal, object, and place had its own guardian spirit that protected it. The spirit of the sky—the Great or Gentle Manitou—watched over the whole world and everything on it. The Sac and Fox always showed respect for the manitous. When they entered a cave or a river, they would thank the cave's or the river's manitou for protecting them while they were there. If a hunter killed a buffalo, he would thank the buffalo's manitou for giving itself to his people.

When confronted by trouble or illness, the Sac and Fox turned to the manitous for advice or a cure. There were many ways to attract the attention of the spirits. One method was to blacken one's face with charcoal. It was also thought that the manitous responded out of pity to those who wailed and fasted. The most reliable way of contacting the spirit world, however, was to smoke tobacco or make an offering of it. The manitous liked tobacco more than anything else, but they could only get it from humans. So if a human offered them some, they were very likely to respond.

Ceremonies and religious observances marked important events in each person's life. When a woman was about to have a baby, she went to a lodge built specially for the birth. Several of her female relatives stayed there with her. If an expectant mother had difficulty giving birth, a woman skilled in healing the sick would be called. In 1918, an elderly Fox woman recalled how a healer had helped her decades earlier:

> When that woman came, she at once boiled some medicine. After she had boiled it, she said: "Let her sit up for a while. You must hold her so that she will not fall over." After I was made to sit up, she spat upon my head; and she gave me the medicine to drink. After she had given me the medicine, she began singing. She started to go out singing and went around the little lodge singing. When she danced by where I was, she knocked on the side. "Come out if you are a boy," she would say. And she would again begin singing. When she danced by she again knocked the side. "Come out if you are a girl," she would say again. After she sang four times in a circle, she entered the lodge. And she gave me medicine to drink. "Now it will be born. She may lie down." Lo, sure enough, my baby was born.

After a baby was born, mother and child remained in the small lodge for 10 days before moving back to their family lodge. When they returned, the parents gave a feast for the baby's oldest relatives, which was attended by many other friends and family members. One of the elderly relatives would

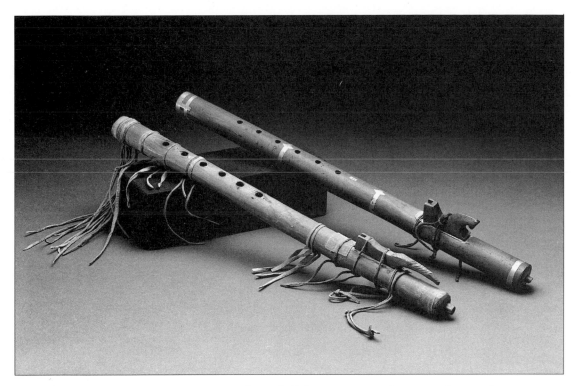

These flutes were made by the Sac and Fox in the 19th century. Music played an important part in tribal ceremonies.

give the child a name chosen from the group of names belonging to the father's clan.

Children spent most of their time playing, but from a very young age they were taught the skills they would need in life. Girls learned to tend the garden, cook, and sew. When a boy was five or six, he was given a bow and some arrows without sharp points. With these, he learned how to shoot at targets. Eventually, he began hunting birds and small animals. Boys also learned to make their own bows and arrows.

When a boy killed his first deer, it was a joyous occasion. Many friends and relatives were invited to a feast to eat the deer, but the boy did not eat any of it. Instead, he listened politely while his father and the guests praised him and predicted great things for his future.

Young boys fasted and kept *vigils* to become closer to the Great Manitou. When a boy reached *puberty,* he went on a vision quest. He would go off alone to pray and fast, hoping for a vision of his own personal manitou. When the vision came to him, he would collect objects such as stones, feathers, and animal claws that signified the power given to him in the vision. Throughout his life, he would turn to that pack of objects when he needed to draw upon that power. Girls also prayed for visions, but they did so at home, not in isolaon.

A girl's passage into puberty was marked by elaborate rituals. When a girl began menstruating, she stayed in a special lodge for 10 days, completely isolated from men. During that time, her mother and other female relatives would visit her, bringing her food and teaching her important lessons about living a proper life and being a responsible and generous adult. At the end of the 10 days, the girl would go to the river to bathe. She then dressed in brand new clothes and returned to her family's lodge. When

When a Sac and Fox girl reached puberty, she spent 10 days in a special lodge while older female relatives instructed her on how to be a responsible adult.

both boys and girls reached puberty, they painted their faces bright red to show that they were adults.

Young men and women usually married when they were about 20 years old. When a man wanted to propose marriage, he would enter the woman's lodge at night. Holding a piece of burning bark, he would go to where she was sleeping, and the two would hold a hushed conversation. If the woman accepted the proposal, she blew out the flame. This meant that they were married. If she did not blow out the flame, the man could try again the next night. If she again refused, the man understood that his proposal had been rejected and he should give up. When proposing to a woman who had previously been married, a man could profess his love by sitting outside her lodge playing a flute, trying to call her out to meet him.

Once a couple was married, their families exchanged gifts in honor of the marriage. If a couple grew unhappy together, they were free to separate and remarry. The Sac and Fox thought that people should never be forced to do anything against their will.

Every Sac and Fox was a valued member of the community, so when someone died, it brought great sadness to the entire tribe. A crier would run through the village, announcing the unhappy event. Then everyone from the dead person's clan gathered for an all-night ceremony mourning the death.

The body was prepared for burial by people outside the deceased's clan. It was thought that the deceased's fellow clan members were so overcome with grief that they were unable to bear the responsibility.

Dead people were dressed for burial in their finest clothes. Bodies were buried with their feet pointing west because it was believed that the spirits of the dead lived in the west. At the funeral, the dead person's relatives placed such objects as clothing, utensils, food, and water in the grave for the deceased to use on his or her journey to the afterworld. The person conducting the ceremony then spoke to the soul of the dead person, advising it neither to look back as it traveled to the afterworld nor to envy those still alive. Next, he sprinkled tobacco in the grave. As the mourners walked past the grave, they also offered up tobacco. A post was erected at the head of the grave and painted with a symbol representing the person's clan.

If the deceased was a warrior who had died in battle, his widow would hang his sacred pack on a bush in front of their lodge. Every day she would sit in the doorway of the lodge, crying and wailing for her lost husband. For the next 15 days, the deceased's friends would come to the lodge to dance. They would also give the widow gifts to comfort her and to show respect for the fallen warrior.

Mourning lasted much longer than 15 days, however. Relatives would mourn for up to a year, during which they followed strict rules of behavior. To show that they were overcome with grief, mourners stopped tending to their appearance. They wore tattered clothes and did not take care of their hair. They avoided dances and other celebrations and hardly ever laughed or spoke. Nor did they work; women stopped farming and men stopped hunting. The Sac and Fox thought that people in mourning could be dangerous to others. For instance, they believed that a mourner's bare foot touching the earth would cause a drought. Thus, mourners wore moccasins at all times, regardless of the weather.

Mourning finally ended when the dead person's clan adopted someone to replace him. This person, usually a friend of the deceased, was chosen by the deceased's relatives. The adoption was celebrated by a feast, games, and dances. The person being adopted and his new relatives also exchanged gifts.

The adoption was only ceremonial. The adoptee did not actually change clans or move into his new family's lodge, but he was symbolically recognized as a member of his new family's clan. After the adoption, the deceased's relatives stopped mourning. This is because they thought the dead person's ghost had so enjoyed the adoption ceremony that it was certain not to become an evil spirit.

The ceremonies marking the different stages of life displayed the sense of community among the Sac and Fox. They behaved with generosity and respect toward both the living and the dead. Their strong social organization ensured that there were few hostilities within the tribe. However, conflict with outsiders was more frequent. ▲

*This painting by George
Catlin portrays the Sac
and Fox battling the Teton
Sioux, with whom they
were often in conflict.*

Chapter 4

Peace and War

Living along the Mississippi, the Sac and Fox came into contact with many other peoples, including British, French, and Spanish traders and such Native American tribes as the Osage, Illinois, Cherokee, Dakota, and Chippewa. Although most of their interactions were peaceful, the Sac and Fox sometimes had conflicts with these tribes that resulted in raiding.

Many raids were carried out for vengeance. If someone from another tribe killed a Sac or a Fox, a member of the victim's family might organize a raid in *retaliation*. When a man wanted to lead a raid, he first fasted, hoping to have a vision in which a manitou would give him advice or a sign of good fortune.

The warrior then built a special lodge and hung a strip of red cloth in front of it. This informed other warriors that the man was planning a raid. If the others wished to join the raid, they would stop in the lodge, smoke tobacco, and discuss plans. Sometimes warriors' wives also went on the raids. The person who built the lodge was the leader of the raid, and he did not need anyone's permission to carry it out.

When the raiding party approached the enemy, the leader rode in front carrying his sacred pack. He kept his pack between his warriors and the enemy at all times. When retreating from a raid, the leader took up the rear so that his pack's power would continue to protect his warriors.

If the raiders were defeated by the enemy, the war party broke up and each warrior returned to the village separately. If they were successful, however, the party stopped outside the village and sent a messenger to announce their victory. When the victorious war party entered the village, they were greeted by dancing and feasting.

Warriors often returned with prisoners captured during the raids. These captives were usually adopted into families that had lost relatives in warfare. The adoptees quickly became regular members of the family and the tribe.

In this George Catlin engraving, a group of Sac and Fox are depicted dressed in war regalia.

Raids were sometimes called because one tribe was using another tribe's traditional hunting grounds. This became more frequent as more and more Europeans settled in the eastern part of North America, forcing the Native Americans who lived there to move west. These types of raids were frequently overseen by war chiefs.

Men who were chosen to be war chiefs had displayed courage in battle and had been successful during raids. Because the Sac and Fox believed that no one should ever be forced to do anything, war chiefs could not *coerce* others into joining their war efforts. Instead, the chiefs had to explain the reasons for the raid and convince warriors to join their war parties. Each warrior then decided for himself whether to go.

War chiefs also supervised the men who functioned as the village police. The main duties of the police were to ensure that people behaved in an orderly fashion and to enforce decisions of the tribal council. The police had the power to destroy the property of anyone who disrupted village life.

Sac and Fox society was very orderly, with little crime and no prisons. The European traders in the area did not lock or guard their storerooms, yet they had no fear of theft. If murder was committed within the tribe, vengeance by the victim's relatives was permitted, but it rarely occurred. More often, the murderer's family gave valuable gifts to the victim's family as compensation.

Most people were discouraged from misbehaving by the fear of losing the respect and friendship of their tribespeople. One family experienced this shame after a divorce. The husband had given a horse to his wife's family during the exchange of gifts that confirmed the marriage. According to custom, the wife and her family were required to return the horse when the couple divorced. However, they refused to give it back. Although the man had the right to retrieve the horse using force, he did not. Instead, he simply had nothing more to do with the family. This was considered a far worse punishment.

In addition to war chiefs, the Sac and Fox also had peace chiefs. Because peace chiefs were wise and even–tempered, tribespeople sought their advice. If a dispute arose among members of the tribe, the peace chiefs met in council to come up with a solution. But as with the war chiefs, peace chiefs could only recommend action to their people. They could not force their will upon anyone.

The councils of peace chiefs also handled treaties and alliances with other Native American tribes, Europeans, and Americans. The peace chiefs discussed the proposed agreements and decided whether the terms should be accepted. When the tribal council came to an agreement, a crier announced the decision in every village.

Women could not be chiefs, but they did influence their communities. Women gave speeches and took part in discussions at public meetings, voicing their opinions and giving advice on matters of importance.

This loose system of government based upon respect, honor, and personal freedom served the Sac and Fox well throughout most of their history. But as their interactions with non-Indians increased, their world would be upturned. ▲

Chapter 5

Time of Trouble

By the end of the 18th century, the Sac and Fox were comfortably settled in their homes along the Mississippi. Their most common trading partners were the Spanish, who had built a large trading post at St. Louis in what is now Missouri. The Sac and Fox frequently traveled there to trade furs and excess corn for metal goods, guns and ammunition, and horses. This trade was beneficial to both sides, and they got along well.

But times were changing. The United States had recently gained independence from Great Britain. The young nation was still just a small cluster of states along the eastern seaboard, but the country was expanding westward with little regard for the Native Americans who were already living there.

United States officials did acknowledge that the Indians held title to the land, and they persistently tried to convince the Indians to sign treaties giving up their territory. During the early 19th century, the U.S. government repeatedly attempted to move the Sac and Fox west of the Mississippi River.

In 1804, a group of Indians, including two Sacs, became involved in skirmishes in which several American settlers were killed. The U.S. government wanted to punish the Indians responsible for the deaths. In an effort to restore peace, the Sac sent four representatives to St. Louis bearing gifts to compensate for the settlers' deaths, as was their custom. But rather than accept the offer, William Henry Harrison, the governor of the Illinois and Indiana territories and future U.S. president, insisted that they pay for the deaths by forfeiting some of their land.

Harrison coerced the four Sacs into signing a treaty giving up all Sac and Fox land east of the Mississippi—in what is now Illinois, Missouri, and Wisconsin—in exchange for an annual payment of $1,000. According to the treaty, the Sac and Fox could stay on the land as long as it was owned by the U.S. govern-

In 1828, Governor William Henry Harrison ordered the Sac and Fox to leave Illinois.

ment. But once it was sold to settlers, the Indians would have to leave.

When the four representatives returned to their village, the Sac and Fox were outraged at what had happened. The four were wearing new coats that U.S. officials had given them, and they appeared to have been drinking heavily. Many people in Saukenuk believed that Harrison had *deliberately* gotten them drunk and bribed them to sign the treaty. Moreover, the treaty had been written in English, which none of the four could read. They had been forced to rely on a translator to tell them what they were signing, but he had not explained how much land they were giving away. Regardless, the treaty was not valid to the Sac and Fox because the four representatives did not have the authority to sell the land. Only the tribal council had that authority, and all treaties had to bear the signature of many different chiefs. When the tribal council met to discuss the terms of the treaty, they all agreed it was not acceptable.

In the next few years, more and more American settlers streamed into Sac and Fox territory. The U.S. Army frequently built forts in newly settled areas because the newcomers were afraid of the Indians. One such post was Fort Armstrong, which was built on

Rock Island very near Saukenuk. The Sacs were outraged that a fort was built right in the middle of their territory, but the U.S. government paid no attention to their protests. As the settlers took over more of their land, Sac and Fox hunters were forced to travel farther north and west in search of buffalo. Eventually, their expeditions took them to the traditional hunting grounds of their longtime enemies, the Teton Sioux, resulting in frequent skirmishes between the two groups.

Newcomers continued to arrive. By 1828, there were around 150,000 white settlers in Illinois—so many that the governor ordered all Indians to leave the state. The Sac and Fox were told to move across the Mississippi River to Iowa and rebuild their villages there. The U.S. government planned to sell their land to settlers. The Treaty of 1804 had been put into action.

Most of the Foxes agreed to move to Iowa. Many of the Sacs also went, but some refused to abandon their homes. This group was led by a man named Black Hawk. Black Hawk believed that land could not be traded as one would trade a coat or a rifle. According to Sac beliefs, "Land cannot be sold. The Great Spirit gave it to his children to live upon, and cultivate, as far as is necessary for their subsistence; and so long as they occupy and cultivate it, they have the right to the soil."

Black Hawk and his followers went on their normal winter hunting expeditions that year. But when they returned to Saukenuk in the spring of 1830, they found that settlers had moved into their lodges and planted crops in their fields. The newcomers had also eaten the Sacs' food that had been stored for the winter. These whites had not even bought the land from the government. They were squatters—people who brazenly moved onto land and began using it as if it were theirs, driving off anyone else who claimed it. The squatters would neither allow the Sacs to enter their own homes nor give them their supply of seeds to plant crops.

Black Hawk protested to American officials about the squatters, but the squatters were also complaining about being threatened by the Indians. Disgusted, Black Hawk later said, "We acquainted our agent daily with our situation and hoped that something would be done for us. The whites were complaining at the same time that *we* were *intruding* upon *their rights! They* made themselves out the *injured* party, and *we* the *intruders* and called loudly to the great war chief to protect *their* property! How smooth must be the language

When Black Hawk and his followers reentered Illinois, Governor John Reynolds called on the militia to remove the Sacs "dead or alive."

of the whites, when they can make right look like wrong, and wrong like right."

Of course, U.S. officials sided with the squatters, but Black Hawk would not give up. He decided to force the squatters out of Saukenuk himself. He discussed the problem with other tribes, including the Winnebago and the Potawatomi, who agreed to help. Some British officials in Canada also promised aid.

So in the spring of 1831, Black Hawk and his followers again returned to Saukenuk. They did not constitute a war party; many of the 500 Sacs were women and children. Nevertheless, John Reynolds, the governor of Illinois, described Black Hawk's return as an "invasion of the United States." Reynolds called up a *militia* of 700 men and ordered them to remove the Sac to the west side of the Mississippi, "dead or alive."

General Edmund P. Gaines, the U.S. Army commander in the area, met with Black Hawk and tried to convince him to retreat. Black Hawk would not relent. On June 25, 1831, the militia descended on the Sac village. But when they got there, there was not a Sac in sight. Sac scouts had heard of the plan, and everyone had safely crossed the Mississippi under cover of night. Angered that the Indians had *eluded* them, the militia destroyed the village and burned all the Sacs' crops.

West of the Mississippi, Black Hawk waited for the help promised by the Winnebagos. It never came. Without more warriors, he had no chance against the army. So when Gaines again offered to negotiate, this time Black Hawk was willing. In the resulting treaty, the Sacs agreed to move permanently to the west side of the river.

continued on page 57

ART IN EVERYDAY LIFE

Creating beautiful artwork has always been a vital part of Sac and Fox culture. Even objects that were made for practical uses—from weapons to storage containers—were colorfully decorated. They were made from animal skins, feathers, plant fibers, wood, and stone and were colored with dyes made from plants. When the Sac and Fox encountered white people, they began using European goods to create their traditional designs. Colored beads, woven cloth, and metal replaced natural materials. White people also made goods for trade with the Indians, such as the tomahawk shown on this page. In spite of the influence of Europeans, the Sac and Fox continue to create designs that reflect their creative heritage.

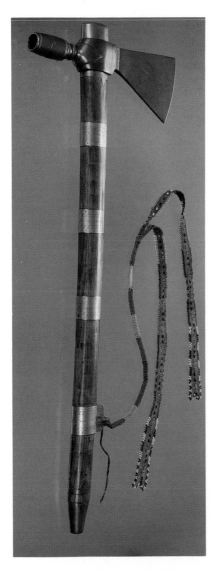

This pipe tomahawk was manufactured by whites in the mid–19th century for trade with the Indians. The head was made of brass, the bands of pewter, and the handle of wood, which could be branded by the owner with individual designs.

On these pages are bandolier bags, which would be worn over the shoulder and might be used to carry powder, ammunition, tobacco, or religious charms. The bags were made of wool and cotton cloth, glass beads, silk ribbon, and yarn. The various designs probably depicted forces, spirits, or powers from the natural world, such as those controlling the winds, the seasons, or various animals.

52

These bags illustrate the way in which form and beauty was integrated in Sac and Fox material culture. The trunk at lower left was made from rawhide and pigment, while the two storage bags displayed were crafted from wool yarn, nettle fiber, and buckskin.

This headdress was known as a roach and was a special mark of status for Sac and Fox warriors. Most often, such roaches were fashioned from hair taken from the tail of a deer and eagle's feathers. The roach was affixed to a small tuft of hair on the crest of a warrior's head, which was otherwise shaved virtually bald.

Made of otter skin and a bear claw, this headdress was also worn by Sac and Fox warriors and was considered a status symbol.

The body and feathers of a bird were used to make this fan.

continued from page 48

During the winter, Black Hawk again contacted other tribes seeking their assistance. He believed that if the Indians worked together, they could force the newcomers off their land. Encouraged by several other tribes, Black Hawk decided to try one last time to return to Saukenuk.

In April 1832, Black Hawk and 2,000 of his followers, including about 500 warriors, again crossed to the east side of the Mississippi. But the support Black Hawk was expecting from other tribes and from the British again failed to materialize. Only a few warriors arrived. The American military, meanwhile, was amassing a force of around 2,000 troops to repel the Indians.

After a short time, Black Hawk realized he had no choice but to retreat. No more allies were going to arrive. His followers had been moving constantly for a month. They were running short of food and had been unable to plant crops. The American troops who were following them were getting closer. Black Hawk had to surrender.

When scouts brought word that a camp of between 300 and 400 troops under the command of Major Isaiah Stillman was nearby, Black Hawk sent three young men with a white flag of truce to the camp. He sent five others after them to watch the proceedings from afar. When the Indians entered Stillman's camp, the soldiers panicked and began firing on them. Four of the eight Sac warriors were killed. The other four fled back to their camp with the horrible news.

Black Hawk was furious that his peace party had been attacked. Knowing that American forces would soon attack the Sacs' camp, Black Hawk and about 40 warriors hid themselves and prepared to fight. When Stillman's troops approached the camp, the Sac warriors sprang from their hiding places, shouting fearsome war cries. Stillman's troops vastly outnumbered the Indians, but they were not prepared for the attack. Convinced that they were surrounded by Indians, they ignored Stillman's commands, turned tail, and fled. Black Hawk was astonished by the whites' frantic behavior at the battle that would be forever known as Stillman's Run.

As American soldiers retold the story of the battle, the number of Sacs became exaggerated. Although there had actually been only about 40 Sac warriors, in the minds of the whites that number was multiplied many times over. Settlers in the area began to panic. Tensions increased and there were alarmed calls for putting an end to Black Hawk's rebellion. A huge militia—over 3,000 troops—was assembled to assist the regular soldiers in the area.

These measures were unnecessary, however, because Black Hawk was not interested in fighting. His people were starving and many were ill. He hoped that if they could make it back across the Mississippi into Iowa, the soldiers would leave them alone.

But on July 21, the army caught up with the Indians as they tried to cross the Wisconsin River. Sac warriors held off the soldiers while the women, children, and elderly crossed the river. Although Black Hawk later claimed that only six of his people were killed, other reports put the number as high as 70. Others were taken prisoner by the soldiers. General Joseph Street noted the pitiful condition of those who were captured, saying, "The prisoners are the most miserable looking poor creatures you can imagine. Wasted to mere skeletons, clothed in rags scarcely sufficient to hide their nakedness, some of the children look as if they had starved so long they could not be restored."

The Sac and Fox who eluded the army continued to flee west. By August 1, they reached the point in western Wisconsin where the Bad Axe River flows into the Mississippi. As Black Hawk prepared to cross the river, he noticed the *Warrior,* a gunship

full of soldiers, downriver. Deciding to surrender, Black Hawk raised a white flag and requested to come aboard the ship.

Instead of accepting his surrender, the ship opened fire on the Indians. Nearly 30 Sacs were killed, and the rest fled into the woods to hide. All through the night, the *Warrior* patrolled the shore, shelling the ragtag band of Sacs. The following day, the army that had

On August 1, 1832, white soldiers massacred about 200 Sac men, women, and children as they fled across the Bad Axe River.

been chasing the Sacs arrived at the bluff overlooking the river. The Sacs were trapped and defenseless. They had no choice but to try to cross the river. Black Hawk later described the massacre:

> Early in the morning a party of whites, being in advance of the army, came upon our people, who were attempting to cross the Mississippi. They tried to give themselves up—the whites paid no attention to their entreaties—but commenced slaughtering them! In a little while the whole army arrived. Our braves, but few in number, finding that the enemy paid no regard to age or sex, and seeing that they were murdering helpless women and little children, determined to fight until they were killed! As many as could, commenced swimming the Mississippi, with their children on their backs. A number of them were drowned, and some shot, before they could reach the opposite shore.

General Street, who was in the advancing army, described the scene similarly, writing, "The Indians were pushed literally into the Mississippi, the current of which was at one time perceptibly tinged with the blood of the Indians who were shot on its margin and in the stream. It is impossible to say how many Indians have been killed, as most of them were shot in the water or drowned in attempting to cross the Mississippi."

Most estimate that some 200 Sacs—men, women, and children—were killed. Black Hawk, however, escaped to a nearby Winne-

bago village where he arranged to surrender to General Street. This ended what is now called the Black Hawk War, the last major Indian uprising east of the Mississippi.

As Black Hawk was being brought to the army post where he would be imprisoned, he reflected on what had happened. He later recalled:

*The Black Hawk War
ended with Black Hawk's
surrender at Prairie du
Chien, Wisconsin, on
August 27, 1832.*

On our way down, I surveyed the country that had cost us so much trouble, anxiety, and blood, and that now caused me to be a prisoner of war. I reflected upon the ingratitude of the whites, when I saw their fine houses, rich harvests, and every thing desirable around them; and recollected that all this land had been ours, for which me and my people had never received a dollar, and that the whites were not satisfied until they took our village and our grave-yards from us, and removed us across the Mississippi. ▲

Chapter 6

Pushed West

In the aftermath of the Black Hawk War, the Sac and Fox were forced to *cede* even more land to the United States. Government officials demanded that they sell a strip of land 60 miles wide along the west bank of the Mississippi. Although the Sac and Fox resisted, they ultimately had to consent. For this 6 million acres of land, the Sac and Fox were paid $60,000 over the course of 30 years, even though the land was worth more than $7 million at the time.

Although the Sac and Fox were now in Iowa, where the United States wanted them, they were still not safe from white intrusion. Settlers were streaming into Iowa, which had

excellent farmland. The Sac and Fox knew that there was no way the American government would let them remain on such fertile land. One Sac leader noted sadly, "We are unable to end the great fog of white people which is rolling toward the setting sun."

Throughout the 1830s, the Sac and Fox were pushed farther and farther west and

When the Sac and Fox were forced out of Saukenuk, many moved to the Iowa River Valley, shown here in an 1844 painting by J. C. Wild. They were eventually forced off this land as well.

forced to cede more and more land. Finally, in the Treaty of 1842, the United States demanded that the Sac and Fox leave Iowa. By 1845, they were to move west of the Missouri River into what is now Kansas.

The Sac and Fox who settled in Kansas had been battered by the deprivation of the previous decades. Their increased contact with non-Indians had brought diseases such as smallpox and measles into their midst for the first time. Because whites had long been exposed to these diseases, their bodies had built up natural *immunities* to them. The Indians, however, had never encountered these diseases, so their bodies had no resistance to them. The Sac and Fox experienced epidemics in which a huge number of people became sick and many died. In 1833, there had been about 6,000 Sac and Fox. By 1846, there were only 2,400.

Life in Kansas was not easy. It was difficult to turn the dry prairie into productive farmland, and the harvests did not yield enough food for all the people. Nor were there enough animals for the men to hunt. The Sac and Fox were reduced to relying on the meager provisions given to them by the U.S. government.

In the early 1850s, about 100 Foxes left Kansas and returned to Iowa. They had been

frustrated by the way of life in Kansas. They also felt that the United States had unjustly punished the Fox for the Black Hawk War, during which the Fox had remained *neutral*. This *renegade* band of Foxes ignored the requests of both their fellow tribespeople and the U.S. government that they return to Kansas. Instead, they bought some land near Tama, Iowa, and established a settlement called Mesquakie.

The Sac and Fox who remained in Kansas were still not secure in their homes. In the

At this meeting in 1867, Sac and Fox leaders agreed to sell their land in Iowa to the U.S. government in exchange for a reservation in Oklahoma.

1860s, they were forced to move to a reservation in Indian Territory—the present-day state of Oklahoma. Indian Territory had even drier land than Kansas and produced even worse crops.

The traditional culture of the Sac and Fox was under constant attack. In 1887, the U.S. Congress passed the General Allotment Act. This act stated that Indian lands were to be divided into parcels of 160 acres per family and 80 acres per person living alone. Any land left over after the allotment would be sold to settlers. Dividing up the land was completely contrary to Sac and Fox ideas of land ownership. In their society, no one person could own land; it belonged to the people as a whole. But the government insisted that the Sac and Fox adopt the custom of individual land ownership.

The U.S. government tried to change other aspects of Sac and Fox culture as well. It built boarding schools on the reservation, separating children from their families so that they could be taught to live like whites. These schools taught skills such as building fences, tending cattle, and sewing. The Sac and Fox disliked this emphasis on manual labor, as well as the militaristic living conditions in the school dormitories, so few parents sent their children to these schools.

Most of the teachers at the boarding schools were missionaries, people who try to convert others to their religion. These teachers wanted the Sac and Fox to give up their traditional beliefs and become Christians. The missionaries had little success, however, as the Sac and Fox clung to the beliefs that had always served them well. Long into the 20th century, half the Sac and Fox people continued to practice their traditional religion.

After all the difficulties and upheavals of the 19th century, the Sac and Fox struggled valiantly to adjust to their new circumstances. They strived to maintain their old way of life and create stability for their families. But as the 20th century progressed, economic hardships continued to plague them. Living conditions were harsh. Their homes were often without running water, heat, or electricity. There was little medical care or educational opportunities.

Most of the Sac and Fox were unable to produce enough food on their allotted land, and they had no money to buy better equipment. To earn money, many sold their allotments to white ranchers or farmers. But after the money they received for the land ran out, they had to find work to survive. Jobs were scarce; most worked as laborers on farms occupying land that the Sac and Fox had

Sac and Fox athlete Jim Thorpe won two gold medals at the 1912 Olympics and later became a star in the National Football League. He is considered one of the greatest athletes of all time because he excelled in every sport he tried.

once owned. Even today, unemployment remains a major problem for the Sac and Fox, reaching 59 percent in Oklahoma in 1991.

Some members of the Sac and Fox community have achieved extraordinary accomplishments despite such hardships. Perhaps the most famous Sac and Fox was Jim Thorpe. In 1950, an Associated Press poll of sportswriters named him both the "Greatest Athlete of the Half-Century" and the "Greatest Football Player of the Half-Century." Thorpe was the hero of the 1912 Olympics, winning gold medals in both the pentathlon, which consists of 5 track-and-field events, and the decathlon, which consists of 10 track-and-field events.

But Thorpe became engulfed in controversy the following year when it was revealed that he had played professional baseball in 1910. At that time, only amateurs—athletes who are not paid—were allowed to compete in the Olympics. Thorpe argued that he had only played minor league baseball for a short time one summer and that he had not received a regular salary, so he had not violated any Olympic rules. But he was judged a professional and stripped of his gold medals. This decision was not reversed until 1973, 20 years after his death. Only in 1982 were his gold medals returned to his family.

Native American children dress in traditional clothing at a powwow in Mesquakie, Iowa, a Sac and Fox settlement established in 1856.

Today, a statue of Black Hawk looms over the former homeland of the Sac and Fox.

In the mid–19th century, there were as few as 1,200 Sac and Fox left, but by 1990 their population had rebounded to over 5,300. While most Sac and Fox participate fully in American society, many also maintain aspects of their traditional culture. In the Mesquakie settlement in Iowa, for instance, many Sac and Fox religious ceremonies continue to be followed, including clan rites associated with the sacred packs. Many people in Mesquakie can also still speak the Fox language.

The Sac and Fox remain proud of their society. They are particularly proud of Black Hawk, who tried so hard to defend their home. In Rock Island, Illinois, a 50-foot-high stone statue of the great leader gazes out over the beautiful valley where Saukenuk once lay. This statue reminds contemporary Sac and Fox and non-Indians alike of the peaceful civilization that once thrived there. ▲

GLOSSARY

cache   something that is hidden away to be used at a later time

cede   to surrender a piece of land to another group

coerce   to use force or threats to make others obey one's commands

deliberately   done on purpose with an understanding of the consequences

elude   to cleverly avoid

forerunner   one that comes before

immunity   the body's ability to resist disease

indulge   to take great, unrestrained pleasure

manufactured   produced by modern methods

militia   a volunteer army that is assembled only for emergencies

neutral   not taking part in a conflict between other people or groups

prosper   to succeed in attaining everything one needs to live

puberty   the time of life when a child's body begins to change into an adult's

renegade   one who refuses to obey the rules of the community and strikes out on his or her own

retaliation   revenge

skirmish   a minor outbreak of fighting

vigil   a period during which one sits quietly and reflects on spiritual matters

CHRONOLOGY

mid-1600s   Iroquois Indians begin moving into Sac and Fox territory in Michigan; the Sac and Fox relocate to Wisconsin

1733   After being attacked by the French, the Sac and Fox settle along the Mississippi and Rock rivers in Illinois and southern Wisconsin

1804   The Sac and Fox sign a treaty with the U.S. government in which they give up their land east of the Mississippi

1828   The governor of Illinois orders all Indians to leave the state; many Sac and Fox move to Iowa; others, including the Sac leader Black Hawk, remain in Illinois

1830   While the Sac are in their winter hunting camps, white settlers take over the Sac village of Saukenuk

1831   Black Hawk and 500 Sacs return to Saukenuk; the militia is sent to remove them, but the Sac flee across the Mississippi into Iowa

1832   Black Hawk and 2,000 followers return to Illinois, resulting in the Black Hawk War and the massacre of 200 Sacs at the Bad Axe River; Black Hawk surrenders, and all Sac and Fox remaining in Illinois move to Iowa

1842   The Sac and Fox are forced to sign a treaty in which they agree to leave Iowa and move to Kansas

1850s   About 100 Fox Indians return to Iowa and establish a settlement called Mesquakie

1860s   The U.S. government drives the Sac and Fox out of Kansas and onto a reservation in Indian Territory

1912   Jim Thorpe, a Sac and Fox athlete, wins two Olympic gold medals

INDEX

ABOUT THE AUTHOR

MELISSA McDANIEL is a freelance writer and editor living in New York City. Her other books for children include *The Powhatan Indians* and young adult biographies of Stephen Hawking and Andy Warhol.

PICTURE CREDITS